WHATEVER THE SEA

FIFE

Please return or renew this item before the latest date shown below

Renewals can be made
by internet   www.fifedirect.org.uk/libraries
in person   at any library in Fife
by phone   03451 55 00 66

AT FIFE
LIBRARIES

ry

D1634889

WHATEVER THE SEA

Scottish poems for growing older

foreword by
Sally Magnusson

compiled and edited by
Lizzie MacGregor

Scottish **Poetry** Library

Polygon

First published in 2016 by
The Scottish Poetry Library
5 Crichton's Close
Edinburgh EH8 8DT

and

Polygon, an imprint of Birlinn Ltd
West Newington House
10 Newington Road
Edinburgh EH9 1QS

www.scottishpoetrylibrary.org.uk
www.polygonbooks.co.uk

ISBN 978 1 84697 338 3

Typeset in Verdigris MVB by 3btype.com

Printed and bound by TJ International, Padstow, Cornwall

The publishers acknowledge investment from Creative Scotland
and are grateful for the support of the Baring Foundation
as part of its 'Late Style' artist commissions.

The petals may fade
like us
but the heart
stays green.

'In terms of a red rose picked at dawn'
from *Amorous Greetings* by Gael Turnbull

Contents

old age blues

as time draws near

Foreword

I opened this marvellous collection at a delicate time. I was still reeling from the trauma of handing over my brand new senior railcard for the first time, hoping against shaming hope that the ticket inspector would look at me, look at it, raise an inquiring, lightly flirtatious eyebrow and murmur, 'Surely some mistake, madam?'

He did not.

Last week I held up the queue in a café while rummaging in my bag for my glasses. Goodness, even the word 'rummaging' conjures a vision of such antiquity that I feel quite faint.

So I confess I approached the poems here with a degree of foreboding. Really, did I want to know how much worse it gets? Was this going to be like childbirth, where everyone feels obliged to let you know what you've got coming? A poetic version of my dear old father-in-law, whose refrain as he creaked himself out of a chair was ever, 'Don't get old, lass. Don't get old'?

The delight of this collection is that it's not like that at all. The poems don't lecture, or grumble, or complain (much), or warn. With wit and wistfulness and sometimes a little sorrow, they explore the never-ageing human heart in its encounter with mortality. And they do it beautifully.

Alan Hill sets the tone in the very first poem with such an arresting image that I can't get it out of my head. He describes the slow, strange discovery that:

> age has drifted down,
> imperceptibly, like dust,
> and you're totally covered.

It's the first of many memorable evocations of time, an understandably persistent theme and the subject of some lovely meditations. Stewart Conn thinks of playing the trout as he fishes ('hard to know / where the river ends and the sea begins'). Ian Hamilton Finlay's metaphor is a ship with leaking hull but scarlet sails. Hamish Whyte sketches an old couple settling into a train table with facing seats, capturing their whole life's journey together in five lines. Lyn Moir's rollicking, grateful 'Last Chance Saloon' is a place where I wouldn't mind joining her.

The collection is blessedly low on sentimentality. I confess to finding it difficult to be all that sanguine about old age after watching the horrors of dementia overtake a parent. Perhaps that's why I like the stringency and simplicity of Helen Cruickshank's:

> Bide the storm ye canna hinder,
> Mindin' through the strife,
> Hoo the luntin' lowe o' beauty
> Lichts the grey o' life.

There are bleaker meditations for sure – even quite a long section candidly entitled 'old age blues'. But many are pleasingly bracing. I love 'Good Old Days' by Elma Mitchell, which catches in the most winsomely wry way how out of kilter the process of physical degeneration feels. After wittily detailing the dire catalogue from the neck down ('Shin repeats to shin, / Welcome, death, you may come in'), she concludes:

> But up here, at the top of the spine, behind the eyes,
> Curtained a little, but not blind,
> Sits a young and laughing mind
> Wondering which part of me is telling lies.

That note of bracing honesty and dark humour is sounded in many different poems. Anyone tempted to compare constipation remedies will certainly think again after reading 'Let Me Not', Pauline Prior-Pitt's barbed manifesto, beginning: 'Let me not be tempted / to talk incessantly about my illnesses'.

Sorrow, the sorrow that comes to every life, is here too. It is quietly put in its place by Iain Crichton Smith, who tells how 'Sorrow remembers us when day is done', but concludes, 'After a while we have to stop listening'.

Self-pity is also shown the door in these poems, and I'm glad of it. Growing older may be a sair fecht much of the time, but life is precious. Many people have longed for the opportunity to wrestle with old age and never got the chance; many would gladly put up with deaf ears and any number of stiff joints to live a few years longer. Ageing is what we concede in return for the joys and sorrows of living at all. That's the bargain.

In Alastair Reid's poem of that name he describes 'weathering' as 'an equilibrium / which breasts the cresting seasons but still stays calm / and keeps warm.'

> Weathering. Patina, gloss and whorl.
> The trunk of the almond tree, gnarled but still fruitful.
> Weathering is what I would like to do well.

This collection weathers us all nicely.

Sally Magnusson

age has drifted down

'That is a strange day'

That is a strange day
when you wake to discover
age has drifted down
imperceptibly, like dust,
and you're totally covered.

Alan Hill

Tide

On that sinuous passage from infancy
and youth's buoyancy through middle
life to advanced years, the one certainty
is a gathering of momentum consistent
with time's flow – something scarcely
uppermost in my mind as the trout
I'm playing draws me downstream
till rocked by the tidal undertow I fight
to retain my balance: hard to know
where the river ends and the sea begins.

Stewart Conn

Haiku

obituaries

for people younger than you

in the daily news

Pauline Prior-Pitt

Còdaichean

Cho faisg 's a tha mi air còd ùr:
còd na h-aoise.

Tha an còrr dhe na còdaichean
snaidhmnichte mum thimcheall
mar shnàthlainn cait: m' òige
mum chasan, 's an còd ùr ud
a fhuair mi anns an oilthigh
teann mum cheann, 's mo chridhe
sgaoileadh le còd Chriosd,

's an fheadhainn ud eile
nach fuasgail mi a-chaoidh:
cho maireannach 's a tha Uibhist
a dh'aindeoin 's gun do sgàin an saoghal
(no air sgàth 's . . .)

'S a-nis an tòimhseachan ùr seo air fàire:
cairt-phlastaig son siubhal an-asgaidh,
an òigridh a' coimhead orm mar bhodach,
an crìonadh a-steach mar phàist'.

O Thighearna, thoir dhomh neart do chòd:
gum biodh e, a dh'aindeoin an ro-thomhais,
cho mìorbhaileach ris a' chòrr.

Aonghas Phàdraig Caimbeul

Codes

How near I am to a new code:
the code of age.

The rest of the codes
are tied around me
like a cat's wool: my childhood
wrapped round my legs,
and that new code I found at university
tight about my head, and my heart
bursting with Christ's code,

and those other ones
I can never untangle:
how everlasting Uist is
even though the world has disintegrated
(or because . . .)

And now this new puzzle on the horizon:
a plastic card for free travel,
the young looking on me as an old man,
the folding in like a child.

O Lord, give me the strength of your code:
that it would be, despite the premonition,
as miraculous as all the rest.

Angus Peter Campbell

Thursday

Gave yet another lecture. God, I'm boring.
Said all the same old things I've said before
With touches of 'however-ing' and 'therefore-ing'.
Dear God, it's true, I'm just an ancient bore.

If only I could tap my old exuberance,
High spirits that I plied in days of yore,
Then maybe I would find a kind deliverance
From the curse of being such a bloody bore.

For I'm the model of a modern academic.
I'm absolutely super at ennui.
I'm just stunning when it comes to a polemic,
And boredom's snoredom's what I guarantee.

I'm putting extra pennies in my pension.
Retirement beckons and the garden calls,
That beautiful, botanical dimension
Where boilersuited pensioners scratch their balls.

But I've a problem, and it's called 'work ethic', so
I'll slog on with the daily, dreary toil.
Heigh-ho, heigh-ho, what a lousy way to go,
To work all day then burn the midnight oil.

Douglas Dunn

The Old Nobby

My hull is leaking like a sieve,
The paint is flaking off my hatches,
My heart's not worn upon my sleeve
(But on my sails are scarlet patches.)

Ian Hamilton Finlay

Weathering

I am old enough now for a tree
once planted, knee high, to have grown to be
twenty times me,

and to have seen babies marry, and heroes grow deaf –
but that's enough meaning-of-life.
It's living through time we ought to be connoisseurs of.

From wearing a face all this time, I am made aware
of the maps faces are, of the inside wear and tear.
I take to faces that have come far.

In my father's carved face, the bright eye
he sometimes would look out of, seeing a long way
through all the tree-rings of his history.

I am awed by how things weather: an oak mantel
in the house in Spain, fingered to a sheen,
the marks of hands leaned into the lintel,

the tokens in the drawer I sometimes touch –
a crystal lived-in on a trip, the watch
my father's wrist wore to a thin gold sandwich.

It is an equilibrium
which breasts the cresting seasons but still stays calm
and keeps warm. It deserves a good name.

Weathering. Patina, gloss, and whorl.
The trunk of the almond tree, gnarled but still fruitful.
Weathering is what I would like to do well.

Alastair Reid

well seasoned

A Birthday

I never felt so much
Since I have felt at all
The tingling smell and touch
Of dogrose and sweet briar,
Nettles against the wall,
All sours and sweets that grow
Together or apart
In hedge or marsh or ditch.
I gather to my heart
Beast, insect, flower, earth, water, fire,
In absolute desire,
As fifty years ago.

Acceptance, gratitude:
The first look and the last
When all between has passed
Restore ingenuous good
That seeks no personal end
Nor strives to mar or mend.
Before I touched the food
Sweetness ensnared my tongue;
Before I saw the wood
I loved each nook and bend,
The track going right and wrong;
Before I took the road
Direction ravished my soul.
Now that I can discern
It whole or almost whole,
Acceptance and gratitude
Like travellers return
And stand where they first stood.

Edwin Muir

Upbeat @ Seventy

You have that blithe intake of breath, singularly
keen to startle a new day, release pure melody

that brightens everything; the skip, the unstressed
upbeat hallmarks you, and all the eagerness

you bring, day out, day in, to the turning calendar;
embracing the unforeseen, the routine, humdrum

with as much verve as the novel or the longed-for.
Another birthday is another note, another song

in life's rich repertoire, another chance to look
time in the eye, unblinking; to keep dancing.

Note: the age in the title could be personalised!

Christine De Luca

On Being Eighty

Broad in the beam? More broad in sympathy.
Stiff in the joints? More flexible in mind.
Deaf on the right? New voices from the Left
In politics and art more clearly sound.
Arteries harden? Movements then more slow
Allow more time to contemplate and ponder.
High on the Shelf? Horizons farther grow
Extending faculties for joy and wonder.
Acceptance gained of what one has to bear?
The hard is then become more bearable
And comrade Death himself finds welcome, so
Quite cheerfully towards eighty-one we go.

Helen Cruickshank

At Eighty

Push the boat out, compañeros,
push the boat out, whatever the sea.
Who says we cannot guide ourselves
through the boiling reefs, black as they are,
the enemy of us all makes sure of it!
Mariners, keep good watch always
for that last passage of blue water
we have heard of and long to reach
(no matter if we cannot, no matter!)
in our eighty-year-old timbers
leaky and patched as they are but sweet
well seasoned with the scent of woods
long perished, serviceable still
in unarrested pungency
of salt and blistering sunlight. Out,
push it all out into the unknown!
Unknown is best, it beckons best,
like distant ships in mist, or bells
clanging ruthless from stormy buoys.

Edwin Morgan

Sea Buckthorn

Saut an' cruel winds tae shear it,   *salt*
    Nichts o' haar an' rain –   *sea mist*
Ye micht think the sallow buckthorn
    Ne'er a hairst could hain;   *could never hold fruits*
But amang the sea-bleached branches
    Ashen-grey as pain,
Thornset orange berries cluster
    Flamin', beauty-fain.

Daith an' dule will stab ye surely,   *sorrow*
    Be ye man or wife,
Mony trauchles an' mischances   *troubles*
    In ilk weird are rife;   *everyone's fate*
Bide the storm ye canna hinder,
    Mindin' through the strife,
Hoo the luntin' lowe o' beauty   *burning flame*
    Lichts the grey o' life.

Helen Cruickshank

Old Age

I have, I think, most organs that
I started with. Some shaped by time
foreshortened, elongated, dulled.
I keep at bay time's passage with the thought
this must I do, this might I do, this ought.
Thus never having nothing on my slate
I draw a little, dance a little, write;
and sometimes in the middle of the night
think splendid thoughts which trickle down
to verse. While opera and music still delight;
there's history and nature to explore
and conversation with the worldly wise,
I'm washed by tides like pebbles on the shore.

Old age! Old age?
I'm sorry sir, I fail to recognise
the title on the page.

Rebecca Pine

Hanging On

I'm hanging on to your early days
when you can't wait for me to arrive
for cuddles and tickles and butterfly kisses.

These days when you snuggle up
onto my knee and listen to stories for hours,
me acting my head off doing the voices.

You think I am skilful at cricket,
your bat hits my ball every time,
and I'm really not bad with a football –
no wonder you score all those goals.

I'm amazed when we're hiding and seeking
at the ingenious places you find,
how in Snakes and Ladders and Ludo
you manage to win every time.

I'm not sure about early mornings,
the knocks on my door to come in,
making a tent of my duvet,
letting the cold air in,

wriggling down to the bottom
and wriggling back up again,
and wriggling down to the bottom
and wriggling back up again.

But, I'm hanging on to your early days
before you discover you're too old for me.

Pauline Prior-Pitt

Aquafit

November Friday mornings when the weather's
foul Glaswegian, see me out my bed
by half past nine, racing the traffic to Scotstoun.
I join the usual coven in the pool, ladies past
a certain age, warming up their tonsils.
Teacher arrives, cranks up the music machine,
and off we go, ready or not, to the sound of
'Running Bear', 'YMCA', Aga-doo-doo-doo.
At last, some use for those terrible songs
of our youth. Heads in various shades of
blonde bob along as we all run up to the
deep end, our lop-sided chests, diabetic legs,
plus plus sizes, varicose veins, paying
tribute to all the babies, the sweeties,
the drinks and fish suppers of our lives.
But here we are, out and proud, doing
frog jumps, star jumps, scissors jumps,
running up to the deep end, turning,
jumping backwards, turning.
'Turn, turn, turn,' she says, butter wouldn't melt.
Is she having a laugh? 'I'd like to turn her,'
someone remarks sourly. Giggles erupt.
'Get a woggle,' she shouts, as we all
tread water and those at the back of the class
return to the real business of the morning,
yackety-yak. Sometimes a man drifts across
by mistake, looking for the speed lane, not sure
what's going on, but we're oblivious (almost)
. . . give us a man after midnight and we're away,
heads bobbing again as we all kick in unison.
Teacher cracks the whip. 'Faster, kick those
legs – let me see knees, knees, knees!'
Someone says: 'Catch yer grannie daeing
this, eh?' We're all having a laugh, now,

some lewd joke or other, I can't catch it but
laugh anyway, and it's onto the last stretch,
little jumps, one, two, three, four, and jump
in the air, and 'Well Done' as we clap ourselves
and make our way, jelly-legged, to the showers,
all of us Dancing Queens fighting our Waterloo.

Rosemary McLeish

Women Friends

so

       easy to be with   you are

easy as the ebb
      and flow of tides   you are

easy as melting snow   you are

wise women
     welcome as sunshine
         spreading delight

Pauline Prior-Pitt

The Release

The scaffolding has gone. The sky is there! hard cold high
    clear and blue.
Clanking poles and thudding planks were the music of a strip-down
    that let light through
At last, hammered the cage door off its hinges, banged its goodbye
    to the bantering dusty brickie crew,
Left us this rosy cliff-face telling the tentative sun it is almost
    as good as new.
So now that we are so scoured and open and clean, what shall we do?
        There is so much to say
        And who can delay
When some are lost and some are seen, our dearest heads,
    and to those and to these we must still answer and be true.

Edwin Morgan

A Cairn

As by barren trackway
on a mountain crest
with view of scree and corrie,
ridge and col,
a traveller might pause,
take bearings, cast
in tribute to record:
'A man came here, went on,
left common token, shared
with those who went before
and shall come after.'

Gael Turnbull

us along the way

Caitean air Uachdar Loch Eiriosort

Caitean air uachdar Loch Eiriosort
's an t-anmoch ann,
bha an latha samhraidh fada,
gruth is bàrr a' coinneachadh:
tha an gaol a leanas fada
duilich a chur an cèill.

Ruaraidh MacThòmais

A Ruffling on the Surface of Loch Erisort

A ruffling on the surface of Loch Erisort
at evening,
the summer day was long,
crowdie and cream meeting:
love that lasts long
is hard to put into words.

Derick Thomson

Watching Telly With You

We could go to Paris of course
but not so often. And it might not be quite
as cosy as the sofa, the fire, our slippers,
the zapper. Sometimes mid-morning
I think about it, hankering a little like
the lovelorn do, for that evening lull,
front door locked, feet up, snugged up,
loved up and watching telly with you.

Diana Hendry

Autumn Compensations

Apples on the bending bough,
    Berries on the thorn,
Wheeling gulls behind the plough
    Where stood yellow corn.
Pungent petals, gold and white,
    Bronze and winey-red,
Blow in cottage gardens bright
    Tho' the rose is fled.

Books in cosy littered room,
    Feet in slippered ease,
Silver candles in the gloom,
    Stars in naked trees.
All the talks that daylight slew
    Shyly come again,
While we sit inside, we two,
    Cloistered from the rain.

We are growing old, my dear,
    Who were wild and young,
Wit informed and wisdom clear
    Fall now from your tongue.
Passion's perfume, beauty's flow'rs
    May be past and dead,
But the mellow fruit is ours,
    Good as daily bread.

Helen Cruickshank

Well-worn

I have worn everything you gave me –
The ring, of course, and that absurd string of beads
Reaching to the navel, and your battered shirts
Full of your energy and our many conjunctions.

And I have worn myself – this body, your tent
Of contentment, once your second skin,
Shrunk now, but serviceable, not yet for the scrap-heap.

I have worn, almost to shreds, our tatty jokes,
Ludicrous memories, and our crumpled rags
Of rhythm and phrase, – old hat, but comfortable.

Everything has been worn, nothing worn out.

Elma Mitchell

The Greater Sea

Oor boat is rigged tae face the greater sea,
The day daws blithely whan we must set sail.
Hou aften hae we twa wrocht in the gale,   *struggled*
An waithert aa its wrath tae bear the gree?   *to win the prize*
We stievely grupt the tiller, haund oan haund,   *steadfastly gripped*
Held firmly tae the course that we hud chosen;
Be't sauf bield o the loch, else sea, or ocean,   *safe shelter*
Nae maitter! We wid siccarly mak laund!   *securely*
An mony's the lauch we hud alang the wey,
We caredna dael-a-hate the haund fate gien us,   *never gave a damn*
But made the best o't, kennin fine atween us   *knowing well*
The bonds o luve we hud wid aye haud sway.
Ayont the faur horizon Venus lowes,   *beyond, glows*
The Cosmos beckons tae us; pynt the prow!   *point*

Rab Wilson

The Great Journey

The old couple
board the train
and make for a table
with facing seats.
The woman says
you sit here
and see where we're going
I'll sit there
and tell you where we've been.

Hamish Whyte

Last Chance Saloon

'Set 'em up, kid' was your usual cry
as you sauntered through the door
with a look in your eye and a whisky sigh
and a voice that could sand the floor.

The girls in the back cleared out damn quick
for they knew that you were mine,
and anyone's try for a fuck on the fly
would put their life on the line;

and none of the guys, if they were wise,
would call for a beer or a shot
while you and I measured eye to eye
never moving from the spot.

Now the tankards break as our clawed hands shake,
and our vision's none too clear,
but our eyes still meet though our fingers ache
and what the hell if the beer

is flat or the spirits drip as we sip,
there's no one in the bar,
and who bar us gives a tinker's cuss
if we spill the whole damn jar?

Those days were good, but these are fine,
we cuss, we kiss, and we drink good wine,
just thank the Lord for that, my dear,
thank the good Lord for that.

Lyn Moir

Sonnet On My Wife's Birthday

All the love I have will not take her years away:
All the knowledge given not grant her time release,
Yet one day less impoverishes this great feast
That grew when we together went our way,
Hurrying to meet our newly planted day,
That barely showed above the stony ground
Of our North-East, whose grudging air beat down
The rare freedom that becomes when two are one.
So, when every loss is gain, as every colour, brown,
Or red or tarnished yellow in our life's spectrum,
Shows itself, why should we protest too much
Against the silent pace that makes in us such
Speed, for we have learned to plant our love so strong
Our children's children now take up the song.

George Bruce

It's been

It's been a long time
all the time we've spent
and we've had such times
though sometimes not
and at other times
just no time at all
and all the time
hard to find time
for what does take time,
to tell you
they've been good times
and often, countless times,
beyond that and now
it's that time
when there's less than there was
but still time
and to spare,
time enough,
this time,
which is always
a long time.

Gael Turnbull

To My Love

An affirmation on an anniversary
After Shakespeare

Shall I compare you to an Autumn day?
The seasons, love, have grown more temperate.
Rough winds have shaken us along the way,
The summers gone too far to contemplate.

Sometimes the going was tough but heaven sent
Its suns and moons and stars to gild our days.
Love was always in our element.
The hills of home tug inexplicably

And nights are drawing in as summer fades.
Possessions mean so little to us now.
The seasons cast their shadows in our wake,
As we foregather to renew our vows.

I toast our years together in this sonnet.
This is our special day and you, my love, are in it.

Lydia Robb

old age blues

Blight

Each of us is old
and our brave silks begin
to fall from us. Draw close
in the chapterhouse of skin.

How shall we be glad?
We were young, young – we knew
it would happen as it happens
but not like this. Not to

us, not to the silk-sellers,
the bearers of spice and gold.
Our tales were bright in the telling
but this was not foretold.

Helena Nelson

On the Slope

I cling to the railings as befits my station:
a senior person slipping slowly downhill.

The world no longer our oyster,
gone are the safaris of yesteryear,

the all-night parties, ice-skating
in the blurry light of dawn . . .

But perpetual youth? Think: the sense
of déjà vu, potions for complexion

and performance, the strain
of staying abreast of fashion.

part consolation, the ungrudged ageing
of loved ones, neither left behind

but each meeting the other's eye,
enriched by what they've been through.

Whereas the mind roaming, and all
forgotten, pray for merciful oblivion.

The one sure adage: Bette Davis's
no-shit 'Growing old sure ain't for sissies!'

Stewart Conn

Late Call

Lord, this is pip-squeak calling.
Even with your infinite technology
I expect your line's busy. Therefore
forgive me my witter, tucked up
as I am in my comfy-comfy
with the telly and all its disasters on.
I expect you've seen. I expect
eternity's in Widescreen.

I hardly like to mention my imaginary
ills, the disturbance in my head,
the way I can't live with you or without.
I run out of usefulness. Grow fat
with anxiety. On a fine morning
I rejoice in your mystery. At night
I listen to your silence and despair.
Dread whatever end's in store.

Attend, Lord, those in valid agony.
I'm just one of the whingers –
though perhaps, as an aside,
you could help me to age as beech leaves do,
transparent enough to let sunshine through.

Diana Hendry

Written in response to Psalm 102

Let Me Not

Let me not be tempted
to talk incessantly about my illnesses;
the love of rehearsing them has become too sweet.

And more importantly
let others not be tempted
to talk in intimate details about theirs.

Let us not be led
into the comparing of tablets, sizes, shapes, colours
how many, how often and for how long.

Let us not tell
how shocked the doctor was
when he saw whatever it was he saw.

Let us not go
into minute details
about the prescribing of ointments, injections, bandages.

Let us not discuss
what the consultant said
nor how long we waited to see him.

Finally, when others ask,
even though we're dying to tell them,
let us have the strength
to say, 'I'm just fine'.

Pauline Prior-Pitt

Absent-mindedness

I am forgetting quite a lot these days.
My task-list is gap-toothed; it should run on
Like sequenced lights in a continuous phase
Of movement – but a good few bulbs have gone.

There are these sudden sleepings in my head;
I meant to buy some wine. I was to meet
That man at Johnstone station, but instead
Stood waiting outside Paisley Gilmour Street.

This, I suppose, is absent-mindedness.
Absence – an emptiness. And yet there seems
No space within my thought, and no distress
In finding duties overwhelmed by dreams.

My absent mind is filled with the delight
Of sweet horizons and the heron's flight.

Alison Prince

Forgetfulness

When my memory
was a film library
with a keen curator

who knew precisely
where to find clips
of every word

I wished unsaid,
or deed undone,
to play back to me

on sleepless nights,
I'd have welcomed her
muddling the reels.

But now the curator's
retired, the ordered
shelves are in chaos.

I roam the racks
without a guide
searching for scenes

I've lost. Sometimes,
unable to remember
what I'm searching for,

I find Forgetfulness
kneeling on the floor –
an old woman, pale

and worried as a ghost,
rummaging in a tangle
of shiny black ribbons.

Vicki Feaver

Old Age Blues

I don't know what I used to know.
I don't say that it isn't so,
I've just forgotten. That's a blow.
When you know nothing, then you go.

The world keeps changing, things must grow;
You spend life learning, but it's slow;
Perhaps my status isn't quo.
I don't know what I used to know.

Well, I must watch, not let it show,
Greet the morning, say 'hello';
When you know nothing, then you go.
I don't know what I used to know.

J.B. Pick

When Day is Done

Sorrow remembers us when day is done.
It sits in its old chair gently rocking
and singing tenderly in the evening.
It welcomes us home again after the day.
It is so old in its black silken dress,
its stick beside it carved with legends.
It tells its stories over and over again.
After a while we have to stop listening.

Iain Crichton Smith

Progress

There they are, widows of the professoriate
Tied to their frail routines, but not unfree
Wheeling their shopping zimmers on Market Street;
And octogenarian still-cycling emeriti
Cautious of cobbles and slow-moving cars
Hunting for elusive parking spaces –
Physicists, medics, classicists, astronomers.
Gladly I yield to their seniority,
Their ancient tweeds, their wrinkled faces.
I would *like* to be a venerable sage,
And might be yet, if I can reach that age,
Nodding off over a Loeb in the Library
Half-way through a forgotten declension,
Defeated, yet again, by Livy's prose.
But I gave up my bike ten years ago,
Terrified of traffic on the A91 –
And that was on the pavement. I suppose
That so-called 'progress' overtakes us all –
Superfast fibre, electronic bravado.
Where will it end? That's what I want to know.
It's years since I saw an icicle.

Douglas Dunn

In Retirement

Widowed of my own image
That shone from fellow faces
I watch from envious window
The men whose energies at morning
Are sucked towards the safe corporeal city.

Young men who run on rails, bereft
Of personal intention, don't condemn
The older one immobile in a chair!
You are the playthings: I the pioneer
Of white Antarctica, bloodless and bare.

Elma Mitchell

The Mower

When I was young and miserable
a misfit and a rebel,
almost never out of trouble,
desperate to escape school,
time dawdled.
           But now I'm older
and happier and want it to go slower,
time's an out-of-control mower
careering through the borders
decapitating all the flowers.

Vicki Feaver

Pruning

I dock the dead, the damaged and diseased;
the gnarled and dry come tumbling from the heights
until I stand knee-deep in bits, well-pleased
I've put a few square yards of world to rights.
I clip and crop, encouraging new growth.
My fingers start to ache but still I snap
my Homebase secateurs. I grin as both
the gleaming silver blades expose more sap.
I deftly make the kindest cuts, and take
the part of surgeon, Adam, God. But mend
myself, I cannot. No sharp shears will make
me sprout, or slow my geriatric trend.
So, wrinkling, stiffening, stooping, short of breath,
I spend my weekends saving plants from death.

Jim C. Wilson

Good Old Days

My neck, where love ran
Just under the skin
Is now an old rickety ladder to the brain.

My breasts, a full delight
For child and man,
The setting
To carry rival jewels,
Dangle now untidy,
Unharvested, over-ripe.

The wishbone of my legs
Has changed their wishes' destination,
Shin repeats to shin,
Welcome, death, you may come in.

I should be cheerless
As a crow in winter fields
When the light is going

But up here, at the top of the spine, behind the eyes,
Curtained a little, but not blind,
Sits a young and laughing mind
Wondering which part of me is telling lies.

Elma Mitchell

as time draws near

Èigh Dheireannach

San *Departure Lounge* airson
Barraigh 's Beinn a' Bhadhla,
Cailleach thapaidh leatha fhèin a' feitheamh
Ris an èigh dheireannaich
Agus guth gu h-àrd ag iarraidh mathanais
Leis gu bheil maill' ann.

Bidh a' chailleach ga cromadh fhèin
Is ag ràdh ri neach
Nach eil san làthair fon teanga:

Coma leat, a luaidh!
Cho cinnteach ris a' bhàs,
Thig i uair no uaireigin.

Final Call

In the Departure Lounge –
it's all the one
terminal and zone –
for Lewis and Harris,
a hardy old cailleach waits on
the final call on her own
and a voice out of nowhere
from above apologises for the delay.

The cailleach turns
and says in Gaelic to someone
who's not there, under her breath:

Don't you worry.
Sure as death,
it'll come sometime.

Rody Gorman

Heaven

A croon, a harp, a bonnie sang,   *crown*
Wi' naething tae dee but tak' wir ease,
An' still-an'-on we're loath tae gyang –   *nevertheless, to go*
Dod, but fowk's gey ill tae please.   *people are very hard to please*

J.M. Caie

Timor mortis conturbat me*

Will it give me six months' warning
Or come when least expected?
Will I trip over it one morning
And find myself disconnected?

Will it come on the way to Corstorphine
Or when sitting on the loo?
Will I need a lot of morphine
Will a bottle of brandy do?

Will it happen in broad daylight?
Or wait until it's dark?
Will it come like a lover at midnight
On a necromancing lark?

Will I lose control of my bladder?
Will I lose control of myself?
Will the Lord send down a ladder
And shock the National Health?

Will it start as a minor chill,
Then turn to a nasty cough?
Will it spread everywhere until
Someone has to switch me off?

Is it already growing inside me?
Does it have a date and a time?
Will I know when at last it's untied me?
O what's the use of rhyme?

Diana Hendry

*'The fear of death disturbs me', a phrase from the Catholic Office of the
Dead, was used notably by William Dunbar, the medieval Scottish poet,
in his 'Lament for the Makaris'.

Bucket

Phrases for the end are throwaway.
'Drop off your twig.'
I quite like that –
cock an eye at heaven in mid-song
and just let go,
get picked up by one stiff claw
for the compost bin.

'Kick the bucket' is a different thing.
My bucket brims
with all I've gathered in.
Leaves and the sun,
a dog to lean on when first vertical
and that dizzy moment of knowing,
I am.

In my bucket rests the rage of sex
and the long work of children
then the survival that goes on alone,
enlivened by accumulated stuff
to work on and play with.
Kick the bucket?
An absurd idea.
I defend my bucket
to the death.

Alison Prince

Come and Go

He has chosen, far nearer the end
than the beginning, to live
where, every day, he can watch the land

come and go, each time gleaming as if
it were new made. Sandbars shoulder
into the sun, their whereabouts too brief

to map, never drying out. Under
its pulsing skin the sea echoes
sunlight, shadows the clouds, goes undercover

in mist. What it is to be bodiless,
boneless, to reshape, to fill
with yourself the moulds of coves and bays,

take yourself back. He walks mile
after mile, blanking aches, stays up late
in the blue half-light, resists the pull

of sleep while he can, while his sight
still serves him, before that jerry-build,
his body, can no longer house a spirit
still nowhere near done with the world.

Sheenagh Pugh

Winter in the World

The old lady struggles, footsteps careful, leaving shuffle marks in
    the snow.
No shopping bag, so maybe it's church, and maybe not. Perhaps
    she is out
for a walk, because she can, and the night is spare, and she is
    undiminished,
and harder than bone.

William Letford

The going

'The going is harder'
he advised me
'as one gets older.'
I didn't believe him.
After all, he was old
and the old are like that.

Now I find it easier
if only to believe him.
Much easier. And the going
not downhill, as advertised.
No descent beckons.
One doesn't get 'past it'.
The real climb
comes toward the end.

Gael Turnbull

At the End

When my last song is finished,
And my heart has lost its fire,
When passion is diminished,
And dead is all desire,
I pray with Death there's no belating,
To keep the undertaker waiting.

I have no dread of dying,
But, O, I fear to think
That long I'll be kept lying
Worn out upon the brink,
What time the sexton's spade doth rust,
And he must drink his ale on trust.

Andrew Dodds

End Matter

i   *You're at the postscript stage,** I read.
        What to say but sorry, thank you,
        blessings, praise?

ii   Have you done all you could?
        All that was in you to do?
        Please leave the house tidy.

iii I used to ask, who was I
        to talk about the moon, war,
        the bickering of men in the city?
        But if not me, awkward, inept,
        mostly foolish, who?

iv The furniture of the house needs renewing.
        The furniture of my heart and mind, ditto.

v   Forget purple.
        Think cashmere.

vi What to do with the smallness of my life
        is such an enormous question.

Diana Hendry

*Dennis O'Driscoll

The Way

Friend, I have lost the way.
The way leads on.
Is there another way?
The way is one.
I must retrace the track.
It's lost and gone.
Back, I must travel back!
None goes there, none.
Then I'll make here my place,
(The road leads on),
Stand still and set my face,
(The road leaps on),
Stay here, for ever stay.
None stays here, none.
I cannot find the way.
The way leads on.
Oh places I have passed!
That journey's done.
And what will come at last?
The road leads on.

Edwin Muir

The Traveller Has Regrets

The traveller has regrets
For the receding shore
That with its many nets
Has caught, not to restore,
The white lights in the bay,
The blue lights on the hill,
Though night with many stars
May travel with him still,
But night has nought to say,
Only a colour and shape
Changing like cloth shaking,
A dancer with a cape
Whose dance is heart-breaking,
Night with its many stars
Can warn travellers
There's only time to kill
And nothing much to say:
But the blue lights on the hill,
The white lights in the bay
Told us the meal was laid
And that the bed was made
And that we could not stay.

G.S. Fraser

Struidhealachd

Nuair a bhios mi air leabaidh a' bhàis,
b' fheàrr leam gun rachadh agam air a ràdh
gun do chosg a' bheatha gu h-ait mi
na gun do chaomhain mi fhìn a' bheatha.

Wantonness

When I lie on the brink of death,
I would sooner be able to say
that life had gaily spent me
than that I had scrimped on life.

Meg Bateman

As Time Draws Near

As time draws near
the end of our days
and the plates fall

away from our knees,
let us not be afraid
of the unsponsored dark.

Heavy grave sin
is weighing your head.
There are shining in darkness

panoramas of terror.
Each nightly picture
is God in his ire.

But for us in autumn
let the trees remind us
of our reasonable sequence,

that like birds we travel
from darkness to darkness
briefly through the hall,

where there remains
the clinking of glasses,
the redness of wine,

though we lie starkly
in our effigies
which will not rise,

pen or sword in hand.
It is an achieved grand
tableau that we leave,

say, turning at the door,
putting on a glove,
and entering the sunset's

enormous concert.
Surely that is better
than on stumbling feet

in the warmth of wetness
squalidly survive.
Live O live,

all you young ones
who take our places
in this hypothesis

of sun and cloud.
May it be with pride
we applaud your litheness

in this panorama,
this drama of our days.
O yes with pride

that we step outwards
into the darkness
closing our eyes

on the last flickering page.

It is time to let the birds migrate without anguish
through the skies of the immediate
towards a fated destination.

It is time to turn the blow lamp on dogma
and inhabit this blue.

Iain Crichton Smith

On a Birthday

Time, why are you going so fast?
    I like not furious paces.
Milestones glimmer and then are past,
    White, solemn faces.

I'm coming near to Forever and Ever,
    With its flower and leaf unfalling,
Where you, poor Time, are an ancient measure,
    Fit for a dream's recalling.

And fain am I to turn again,
    Before this journey's ended,
For a long, long look at the road I came,
    So rough and dark and – splendid!

Marion Angus

Biographical notes

MARION ANGUS (1865–1946) wrote in English and in the Scots of her native North-East; her first books were published in the 1920s, making her one of those poets now seen as forerunners of the Scottish Renaissance. She was already over fifty when she started to write poetry, often on themes of social disconnection.

MEG BATEMAN (b. 1959) is a leading authority in Celtic and Gaelic literary studies and an acclaimed poet. A professor in the University of the Highlands and Islands, she teaches at Sabhal Mòr Ostaig on Skye. She has published poetry in parallel Gaelic and English; *Transparencies* (Polygon, 2013) marked a departure, as most of the poems were written in English.

GEORGE BRUCE (1909–2002) Bruce's finely wrought poetry spanned six decades. He was made an OBE in 1984 and at the age of ninety won the Saltire Society's Book of the Year award for his collection *Pursuit*. His collected poems were published under the title *Today Tomorrow* by Polygon in 2001.

J.M. CAIE (1878–1949) Caie's career was in agriculture; he joined the newly formed Department of Agriculture for Scotland, and became its deputy secretary by 1939. A skilful poet in the Doric, he wrote realistically about farming life and seasoned the realism with the wry verses of his 'Cynical Observes'.

AONGHAS PHÀDRAIG CAIMBEUL / ANGUS PETER CAMPBELL (b. 1954) is a poet and novelist, born in South Uist, now living in the Highlands. He has worked as a journalist, writes plays and novels in Gaelic and has published four collections of poetry; *Aibisidh* was published by Polygon in 2011. He was awarded the Bardic Crown at the National Mod in 2001.

STEWART CONN (b. 1936) Poet and playwright, Conn was the inaugural Edinburgh City Makar in 2002. He has more than a dozen collections of poetry; *The Touch of Time: New and Selected Poems* was published by Bloodaxe in 2014. His more recent work explores themes of mortality and celebrates love in maturity.

HELEN CRUICKSHANK did much to promote the twentieth century renaissance of Scottish literature; her autobiography also serves as a memoir of cultural life in Scotland from the 1930s to the 1960s. Despite full-time employment, and writing her own poetry (her *Collected Poems* was published by Reprographia in 1971), she served as Secretary for Scottish PEN during its formative years and helped create a fertile ground for exchanges between writers, publishers and artists.

CHRISTINE DE LUCA (b. 1947) is a native Shetlander who has lived in Edinburgh for many years. She was appointed that city's Makar in 2014 and is an energetic activist for the art of poetry. She writes in both Shetlandic and English and has six main collections of poetry; *Dat Trickster Sun* was published by Mariscat Press in 2014.

ANDREW DODDS (1872–1959) was born into a mining family in Midlothian. He channelled his talent for writing into newspaper articles supporting Labour politics and the work of agricultural unions, and into five books of poetry, from *The Lothian Land* in 1917 to *The Lady April* in 1951, which gave an unsentimental picture of the life of farm labourers.

DOUGLAS DUNN (b. 1942) Dunn was Professor of English at the University of St Andrews until 2008; he has published over a dozen collections of poetry as well as essays and fiction. *New Selected Poems* was published by Faber in 2003. His poems on the themes of ageing, one of the Baring Foundation's 'Late Style' commissions, can be found in the anthology *Second Wind* (Saltire Society, 2015). He was awarded the Queen's Gold Medal for Poetry in 2013.

VICKI FEAVER (b. 1943) is Emeritus Professor at the University of Chichester, now living in Scotland. She has three collections of poetry; *The Book of Blood* was published by Cape in 2006. Her poems on the themes of ageing, one of the Baring Foundation's 'Late Style' commissions, can be found in the anthology *Second Wind* (Saltire Society, 2015).

IAN HAMILTON FINLAY (1925–2006) was a poet and artist whose work is characterised by semantic brevity, inventiveness and wit. He set up the Wild Hawthorn Press in 1961 and created the poetic landscape Little Sparta over three decades from 1970. His own poems, produced in many different forms, often focused on boats.

G.S. FRASER (1915–1980) Scottish-born Fraser saw service in Egypt during the Second World War and thereafter worked as a literary journalist in London and subsequently as a university lecturer at Leicester. His poetry was first published in book form in 1944; a new *Selected Poems* was brought out by Shoestring Press in 2015.

RODY GORMAN (b. 1960) Born in Dublin and now living on the Isle of Skye, Rody Gorman writes in and translates between Irish and Scottish Gaelic. He has been a writing fellow at Sabhal Mòr Ostaig, works as a creative writing tutor and edits the Scottish / Irish poetry magazine *An Guth*. A selection of his poems in both languages was published in *Chernilo* by Coiscéim in 2006.

DIANA HENDRY (b. 1941) grew up in England and settled in Edinburgh some years ago. She is an award-winning children's novelist and has six collections of poetry; *The Seed-box Lantern: New and Selected Poems* was published by Mariscat in 2013. Her poems on the theme of ageing, one of the Baring Foundation's 'Late Style' commissions, can be found in the anthology *Second Wind* (Saltire Society, 2015).

ALAN HILL (b. 1933) Edinburgh resident Alan Hill started to write poetry in his thirties, continued in retirement and has two early collections. *No Biography: Parts of a Life in Tanka* was published by Happen*Stance* Press in 2010 and spans forty years of writing.

WILLIAM LETFORD (b. 1977) graduated with an MLitt in 2008, won a New Writer's Award from the Scottish Book Trust and an Edwin Morgan Travel Bursary and had his first and second collections published by Carcanet: *Bevel* in 2012 and *Dirt* in 2016.

RUARAIDH MACTHÒMAIS / DERICK THOMSON (1921–2012) was Professor of Celtic Studies at the University of Glasgow for three decades, until 1991. Himself a major Gaelic poet, he was influential in shaping the development of Gaelic post-war writing as critic, publisher and editor of the magazine *Gairm*. His first book of poetry was published in 1951, and his last, *Sùil air Fàire: dain ùra / Surveying the Horizon: recent poems*, by Acair in 2007.

ROSEMARY McLEISH (b. 1945) was born in Glasgow, completed a degree in creative writing in her native city in 2005 and now lives in Kent, where she combines her poetry with her artwork for exhibitions. She has been published in several Grey Hen anthologies.

ELMA MITCHELL (1919–2000) Lanarkshire-born Elma Mitchell went south with a scholarship to Oxford and remained in England, working as a librarian for the BBC and latterly as a freelance writer and translator. Her compassionate insights into people's lives were collected in four books of poetry; *People Etcetera: Poems New and Selected* was published by Peterloo in 1987.

LYN MOIR (b. 1934) was born in Glasgow, studied and worked elsewhere in Britain and abroad and returned to Scotland to settle in St Andrews in 2001. She has been a Hawthornden Fellow and has published four collections of poetry; *Velázquez's Riddle* was issued by Calder Wood Press in 2011.

EDWIN MORGAN (1920–2010) became Scotland's first National Poet, or Makar, in 2004. His poetic output was hardly dimmed by increasing age; *Collected Poems* (Carcanet, 1990) and *Collected Translations* (Carcanet, 1996) were succeeded by several later volumes of poetry, including *Dreams and Other Nightmares* (Mariscat Press, 2010). He was awarded the Queen's Gold Medal for Poetry in 2000.

EDWIN MUIR (1887–1959) was born in Orkney, but moved to Glasgow when he was fourteen. His poetic vision is strongly influenced by a longing for lost Edens and lost childhood, as well as by his apocalyptic sense of war and its aftermath. An influential critic as well as poet, he published seven volumes of poetry, collected most recently by Faber in 1984.

HELENA NELSON (b. 1953) Poet and publisher Helena Nelson was born in Cheshire and lives in Fife. She is the founder editor of Happen*Stance* Press, which won the Michael Marks Award for Poetry Pamphlets in 2010. Her second collection, *Plot and Counter-Plot*, was published by Shoestring Press in 2010, and a new edition of the prose guide *How (Not) To Get Your Poetry Published* by Happen*Stance* in 2016.

J.B. PICK (1921–2015) The writer and critic J.B. Pick was the biographer of Neil Gunn and commentator on many other Scottish authors. He produced a series of annual pamphlets of brief poems and aphorisms to send to friends. *Being Here: selected poems 1943–2010* was published by Markings in 2010.

REBECCA PINE ceased roaming the UK in 1982 and settled in Tarbert, Argyll where she runs a poetry group of over twenty years' standing. She has for many years produced an annual poetry diary and has been published in *The Herald* and elsewhere, and in various anthologies.

ALISON PRINCE (b. 1931) is a poet, biographer and prize-winning writer for children who lives on the Isle of Arran. In her recent poetry she confronts ageing and illness and mines the new understandings they bring. Her collection *Waking at Five Happens Again* is published by Mariscat Press and Happen*Stance* in 2016.

PAULINE PRIOR-PITT explores themes of ageing in her poetry, and writes about North Uist, her adopted home. She has published six collections with Spike Press and has produced four handmade pamphlets, the first of which, *North Uist Sea Poems*, won the Callum Macdonald Memorial Award in 2006. *More Precious Than Moons*, about grandchildren, appeared in 2012.

SHEENAGH PUGH (b. 1950) A long-time resident of Wales, Pugh now lives in Shetland. She has published fourteen poetry collections and two novels and has won prizes for her poetry and translations. Her poetry is often concerned with the tenacity of life in difficult circumstances. *Short Days, Long Shadows* was published by Seren in 2014.

ALASTAIR REID (1926–2014) was a poet, essayist, traveller and a consummate translator, instrumental in bringing the poems of Neruda and Borges into English. He worked for over forty years as a foreign correspondent for the *New Yorker*. *Inside Out: Selected Poetry and Translations* was published by Polygon in 2008.

LYDIA ROBB (b. 1937) writes poetry and prose in English and Scots. She has been included in various anthologies, and her collection *Last Tango with Magritte* was published by Chapman in 2001. She has won a handful of prizes, largely for work in Scots, including the Hugh MacDiarmid Tassie.

IAIN CRICHTON SMITH (1928–1998) was born on the island of Lewis and spent most of his life as a schoolteacher in Glasgow and Oban, receiving an OBE in 1980. In his fiction and poetry in both English and Gaelic he viewed Scotland's culture, small communities and religion with a keen eye. *New Collected Poems* was published by Carcanet in 2011.

GAEL TURNBULL (1928–2004) was a medical practitioner in Britain, America and Canada and returned to live in his home city of Edinburgh. His work ranged from prose poetry and collage poems to his inventive 'poem-objects', but all express a 'delight in language and in the possibilities of utterance'. His published poetry is collected in *There Are Words: Collected Poems* (Shearsman, 2006).

HAMISH WHYTE (b. 1947) is a poet, publisher, anthologist and former librarian. He has edited several anthologies of Scottish poetry and contributes to current poetry publishing in Scotland with his award-winning Mariscat Press. His collection *The Unswung Axe* was published by Shoestring Press in 2012.

JIM C. WILSON (b. 1948) Edinburgh-born poet and creative writing tutor Wilson has revisited the 1950s of his childhood in his prose work *Spalebone Days* (Kettillonia, 2002); his poetry often takes a wry look at getting older. *Come Close and Listen* was published by Greenwich Exchange in 2014.

RAB WILSON (b. 1960) is a poet and Scots-language activist, born in Ayrshire. He has three main collections of poetry, has set Omar Khayyam and Horace into Scots and has collaborated with Calum Colvin in a book of responses to Robert Burns. Poems from his James Hogg Creative Residency were published in *Hairst* in 2015.

Acknowledgements

Our thanks are due to the following authors, publishers and estates who have generously given permission to reproduce poems:

Marion Angus: 'On a Birthday', from *The Singin Lass: Selected Works of Marion Angus* (Polygon, 2006), by permission of Polygon; Meg Bateman: 'Struidhealachd' / 'Wantonness', from *Soirbheas/Fair Wind* (Polygon, 2007), by permission of Polygon; George Bruce: 'Sonnet on My Wife's Birthday', from *Today Tomorrow* (Polygon, 2001), by permission of Polygon; Angus Peter Campbell: 'Còdaichean' / 'Codes', from *Meas air Chrannaibh / Fruit on Branches* (Acair, 2007), by permission of the author; Stewart Conn: 'Tide', from *The Touch of Time* (Bloodaxe, 2014) and 'On the Slope', from *Ghosts at Cockcrow* (Bloodaxe, 2005), by permission of Bloodaxe Books; Helen Cruickshank: 'On Being Eighty', 'Sea Buckthorn', 'Autumn Compensations', from *Collected Poems* (Reprographia, 1971), by permission of Miss Flora Hunter; Christine De Luca: 'Upbeat @ Seventy', by permission of the author; Douglas Dunn: 'Thursday' and 'Progress', from *Second Wind* (Saltire Society, 2015), by permission of the author; Vicki Feaver: 'Forgetfulness' and 'The Mower', from *Second Wind* (Saltire Society, 2015), by permission of the author; Ian Hamilton Finlay: 'The Old Nobby', from *The Blue Sail* (Wax 366, 2002), by permission of the Estate of Ian Hamilton Finlay; G.S. Fraser: 'The Traveller Has Regrets', from *Selected Poems* (Shoestring Press, 2015), by permission of Shoestring Press; Rody Gorman: 'Èigh Dheireannach' / 'Final Call', from *Southlight*, 4 (2008), by permission of the author; Diana Hendry: 'Watching Telly With You', 'Timor mortis conturbat me', 'End Matter', from *Second Wind* (Saltire Society, 2015) and 'Late Call', from *Late Love* (Peterloo / Mariscat, 2008), by permission of the author; Alan Hill: 'That is a strange day', from *No Biography: Parts of a Life in Tanka* (HappenStance, 2010), by permission of the author; William Letford: 'Winter in the World', from *Bevel* (Carcanet, 2012), by permission of Carcanet Press; Rosemary McLeish: 'Aquafit', from *Cracking On: Poems on Ageing by Older Women* (Grey Hen, 2009), by

by permission of the author; Rab Wilson: 'The Greater Sea', from
Eiks an Ens, No. 3 (October 2012), by permission of the author.

Every effort has been made to trace copyright holders of the poems
published in this book. The editor and publishers apologise if any
material has been included without appropriate acknowledgement
and would be glad to receive any information on poets and their
estates we have not been able to trace.